I0172793

TOURIST
TOURIST
TOURIST
TOURIST
TOURIST
TOURIST
TOURIST
TOURIST
TOURIST
TOURIST
TOURIST
TOURIST

Tourist

Copyright © 2018 by Bryan Borland

Cover art: *Every Act of Creation Is First an Act of Destruction*
by Eugenia Loli. Used by permission of the artist.

Cover design: Seth Pennington.

All rights reserved. No part of this book may be reproduced
or republished without written consent from the publisher,
except by reviewers who may quote brief excerpts in
connection with a review in a newspaper, magazine, or
electronic publication; nor may any part of this book be
reproduced, stored in a retrieval system, or transmitted in
any form, or by any means be recorded without written
consent of the publisher.

Sibling Rivalry Press, LLC
PO Box 26147
Little Rock, AR 72221
info@siblingrivalrypress.com
www.siblingrivalrypress.com

ISBN: 978-1-943977-49-9
First Sibling Rivalry Press Edition: Spring 2018

This title is housed in the Rare Book and Special
Collections Vault of the Library of Congress.

TOURIST
Bryan Borland

SIBLING RIVALRY PRESS
DISTURB/ENRAPTURE

LITTLE ROCK, ARKANSAS

TOURIST

America I've given you all and now I'm nothing
America when will we end the human war?
When will you take off your clothes?
America why are your libraries full of tears?
America when will you be angelic?
America the plum blossoms are falling.
- Allen Ginsberg, "America"
America it's them bad Russians.
America this is quite serious.
America this is the impression I get from
looking in the television set.
America is this correct?
America I'm putting my queer shoulder to the wheel.

SUMMER IN AMERICA

It's summer in America and no one knows
how high to fly their flag
                              or which flag to fly
for our part we have again pledged allegiance
to one another   but this isn't a love poem
there are no love poems in America today
only the poetry of necessity   of documentation
written at a time when we can make no promises
of life in twenty years   or less than that
if our skin is brown or black   look back
that same number of years to what the poets
were trying to tell us   and who listened
and why we didn't   look at the revolutions
that begin when we remember to point
the camera outside ourselves   the enemy
of our enemy is our enemy is what they
teach us but what does that camera catch
:   the murder in front of our smiling faces
the blood splatter on our shirts
they tried to tell us was decoration

BILLBOARD

Make / America / Great / Again
with the refugees somewhere else.
It takes very little to make
someone a refugee. Fear. Bombs.
Water, too much or not enough.
We all run from something. Now
we are under beds or behind the old
refrigerator, empty stomachs sucked in,
remembering not to breathe too loud.
This is not a dream
but a headline: *we'll pay for*
the wall until they pay for the wall.
How we will pay: missing
bodies at the dinner table. Money
means so much less than you think. This
is not a prediction but the fact
of uncommon American ground.

THE RENTED HOUSE

The pantry full of ants again
the water drips   sometimes I think
we're not supposed to be here
if a house can welcome you
can't the opposite be true
the energy that lingers   not a haunting
exactly but remnants   some love-
less marriage   endless work
stale sex hanging in the air
a door of constant goodbyes   and maybe
that's it   the house knows
we aren't permanent
maybe the same as we plant no garden
it keeps some cabinet doors jammed shut

CHELSEA BOOM

The television burns in the window
we see ourselves   someone complains
of the crowd   the trains not moving
the fall beginning   we should have known
how it all can change   a thousand miles away
you know more than I do   a backpack
a pressure cooker full of nails
this is the America you see on the news
this is the story   you will worry
through the night   even when I call
you from a speeding car   even when
you know I'm safe   you are full of fear
my backpack is full of books

TOWNHOUSE COCKTAIL BAR

The man from London said
Trump was going to win.

He said it had just happened in England,
the trainwreck politick,
and they should have seen it coming.

He said it was like being punched in the face,
that America was about to get hit,
but I didn't believe him.

It was September.

I didn't believe him one bit.

THE HOUR OF COMMON PRAYER

Love   the giants are falling around us
the great columns of certainty   the disappearance
of our teachers   the rise of cruelty in the world outside
the gods we question now answer us with
different voices   perhaps playtime is over
last night two friends we love separated and you
took the midnight call   this morning
you sent them the truth of an old blues song
that timeless guide to shattered glass   we're old
enough now to know storms and pleasures
the miracle intersection of violence and kindness
the bird we've named in early hours and her brutal
hunt for another summer   you and I want
to be smarter   to pay attention
last year's gods: rye / good cheese / other men
this year is the taste of cold water and each other
I tell you twice a day how beautiful you are
I tell you this and more   but I want to love you better
I want to love you better than I can
the gods they change but the prayer remains the same

WHAT ELSE WERE WE TO DO

Suppose fifteen years ago there was romance
the best we could imagine   the best we knew how
or understood   then suppose there was disaster
not natural but manmade   a small town rendition
the mechanisms of frenzy   suppose I was never heard from
again   nor you   suppose it went like this
I brought you coffee   I disappeared   or was taken
black hood blue // dark van red // dirt road
the color of your skin   suppose out of all that
I became the worker   you became the machine
in the machine   suppose we kept our distance
grew into the captains of ourselves
suppose then each of us were drafted to war and
suppose we fought on different sides of the same blood-
wet field   we who are marked with scars on our thighs
in the shapes of one another's fingers   suppose we went
about our living then // suppose we forgot //
but suppose we saw each other one day
suppose it was today   just from a distance
a supermarket or hardware store   a split second
of illogic   suppose it was like seeing
the murdered back alive   after all   we'd held the funerals
after all   we'd forgotten where we once lived
and the turns to get there

TOURIST

You research the stage, the venue before the drive
as much to decide what to wear as what to read.
You learn to do this, which part of your body to cover,
what skin to show for the red carpet or the dirt road,
the slow and easy drawl in the baseball cap
or the literati with the queer scruff and bag.
You do this naked or in drag and sometimes
these terms reverse their definitions
depending on your mood or the weather,
depending on the city. Still the pretty girls will always
smile when you say husband
and this is how the world has changed,
though how many times you say it and in what accent
is measured for presentation. Or protection.
In California you're entertainment.
In Mississippi you're education.
There are still freshmen who've never met
a person who is openly gay and writing about it.
This is mostly in the south, in rural schools
with dry counties and curiosities wet with prohibition.
Then there are classrooms full of students who

don't believe in labels at all, or coming out,
each row of desks a different color
on a spectrum they dreamed after you woke.
There are no lines. They all hold hands.
Across the country you change
the game plan on the fly, the set lists,
asking the audiences if they it want it
dirty or if they want it sweet.
No smiles means you're a missionary poet tonight.
Laughter means you might go home with someone,
end up in their bed, one way or another.
Your books on their floor.
Your words in their head.

CHICAGO

It's a celebration   another kind of riot   this city needs
nothing of statistics   not all marriages end in divorce
the effect of a broken streak is something made stronger
the bar is full of expectation   the bed later is full of boys
one of them wears the colors of the hometown team
another wears nothing   I wear the colors of a traitor
all   blue and red and blue
the only time in eighteen states I share a bed
the entire time   I think of you
the entire time   I think of you
the entire time
I think of you

FESTIVAL POET

I apologize in advance for the name dropping.
I apologize for not keeping a journal and for having
to do it like this, tucking these receipts in my pocket,
knowing on the long walk home
some of them have already gone missing. Instead
I have the pictures I took or didn't take: the Poet
Laureate's arm around my shoulder. Billy Collins sitting
next to me watching Gary Snyder sing the original
British-Drinking-Song lyrics of the Star Spangled Banner.
Anne Waldman rattling the electric unwild who *never have
enough be enough get enough… never have enough be enough.*
Our hotel rooms were full of mirrors. It went to
my head. There were times I didn't recognize
my face. A stranger in the hallway reminded me
my name. I wept when I saw my books stacked for sale.
I bought my own books. I dreamed up everything.
I'm the boy in audience memorizing every word,
the one who asks a question, and who I answer
with a promise I'll write him into this poem.

LOS ANGELES

Everyone here
knows something I don't, how to work
shop a poem, how to fill silence with words
that leave the others nodding in agreement.
I only want to say everything is beautiful,
but I get the feeling saying
everything is beautiful
gets cold, like the coffee I spill over
everyone else's notes. I'm clumsy in
this room. Everyone here knows
what it's like to be right, exactly
what the metaphor means.
Everyone knows that when the poet says
Los Angeles is burning,
she doesn't mean the city.
She means my face.

INDIANA

                    GAY

    my   GRIEF

            my   RAVAGE

    on the bodies of

                    sons

    o   little thing

                    close your eyes

    I   worship

                    a god

                    you would

                            love

WASHINGTON

In the early fall
I walked down the sidewalk
across from the obnoxious hotel
in a city where the monuments are smaller
than the history they carry. Earlier I'd asked
the cab driver if he ever gets used to the enormous.
This was the refrain of the tour.
Are you complacent to this beauty?
What do you still see?
Are you stopped by the way the light falls on the marble
the red of the dirt the blooming oranges on the trees
in the middle of your day your business as usual?
The hotel I think was the only ugly
thing I saw all fall, the gilded palace with
surname as brand.

. . . When you're a writer
I'd tell the audiences along the way
you're the brand it's your story
you're the story sometimes I don't
even read the manuscripts before I say yes

that's the secret that's the trick and the truth
it's the writer it's the person who makes me feel
the hope of creation what bridges
does your story build who's waiting on
the other side to walk across to feel the connection
who feels like a monster who feels alone
whose stories will intersect your own . . .

In November I have to remind myself of this:
Bryan, Bryan, Bryan: If there's a separation
build a bridge. If there's a palace
be the hammer and the spray paint.
If there's a wall
be the hands that tear that fucker down.

IF YOU CAN HEAR THIS

If you can hear this

> you are the resistance
> you are the underground

there is static in the air
the connection isn't stable
there is talk   no longer rumor
of iron walls and white curtains

but if you can hear this

> you are the resistance

get the books you love
you'll need them more than ever
harden your right to memory
you'll need that too
steel your body for the poison
and the antidote
if not bread and water

we must talk in the languages
of poetry and survival

if you can hear this

      you understand

we now must decide what to fight
to protect first
who to hold closest
who to hide

whether to leave the art hanging
in the living room
or bury it for preservation

ORANGE COUNTY

I feed myself to the hungry dark
so I won't wander away from all this.

The next stop is something to hold me down.

There are neon signs outside the window
and purple lights above the bed.

The motel door is half-open.

I sleep half-alone.

SANTA CLARA

In the aftermath
the air is a burden
of passage.

In the lemon tree a single lemon
no one dares pick.

The faculty pickets something
long planned, now with less meaning
in this new country, same
as the old. In the streets every night
there are human fences,
barricades against the barricades
promised to come.

I feel my otherness, my white,
southern maleness like a wet
dress.

On the news
everything is hate; hate
looks like me.

ONE AMERICA COMES TO THE OTHER

I drove a rented white jeep
into the open jaws of the desert
where every year the grass
is dealt such a cruel season
it must be planted again come the next.
In some cities everything is fake
or faked. I don't mean to say it wasn't
gorgeous, or that I didn't love it, or that
I wasn't taken care of. I don't mean to say
I'd never go back;
I would, and I'd take you with me.
What I mean to say is
some islands aren't surrounded by water.
The aftershock of being called faggot
in a Palm Springs Home Depot
travels fast. Like a fire in a house
suspended entirely over a swimming pool,
a spectacular burn so close
to the power that could save it.

PACIFIC

Isn't there something about the ocean

the first moment it comes into view

it's like waking up next to someone you love

or next to someone you have wanted so badly to love

or next to someone you love

but maybe have forgotten you love

or at least forgotten

        you love like this.

SAN FRANCISCO

In San Francisco I dream
I write a poem with the line
Allen sends his regards
because earlier in the dream Allen
sent his regards. I dream this after
I'd spent the afternoon in City Lights
and bought a copy of *The Fall of America* to mourn
the fall of America in the bar next door, the one
with the drink you can order called the Kerouac
with a shot of tequila and a shot of rum and
nothing else that matters much. I dreamed
years ago I gave a reading in an apartment
in the Castro surrounded by boys like me
because living rooms are for the living
and I always dreamed I'd live like that.
Or maybe I wrote a story where that happened
or maybe it actually happened and really
is there any difference between something
we once dreamed about doing and something
we actually did do when both only occupy
some place in our minds?

Allen and his regards exist like this.
He's sitting crossed-legged in a cloud of smoke
when he talks to me but I don't see
a cigarette so I worry for a moment he's
smoldering in the afterlife but he tells me
no it's a ritual to communicate through the void
and it's working just fine not to worry
just get on with the show and write
the damn poem, son. Write the damn poem.

SECOND LEG

It takes a moment to return to you:
the fake air, the time zones, the noise
of everything else. It takes a moment to
remove all the clothes I over pack,
all the falsities I wear
when you aren't there. It takes a sea
change to let that stranger die,
to pry his hand open and let go, let him
evaporate into our living
room, where, in just a day or two,
I'll stand in the open doorway, forgetting
I'm naked, and you'll have to push me
out of view of the neighbors.

BUYING GROCERIES
WITH MONEY FROM POEMS

Someone taught me not to expect money
for this work. Someone taught me to question
whether it is work at all but I rarely do that anymore.
Last night I read poetry for some people.
I signed a few books.
This morning there is money in my pocket.
I've made more in other jobs but can't remember
a thing I ever bought with it. Now
I remember everything: the significance of salt,
of day-old bread softened
with the juice of ripe tomatoes.
My husband loves fresh fruit.
I buy him a bag of the sweetest apples.
Someone taught me not to expect satisfaction.
I want to offer them an apple.
I want to say, *Here. Taste this.*

HOW TO TOUR

Be hungry. Be interested in the state of things,
the mathematical changes of energy as you
interact with each exact moment. Be willing to
untangle yourself from cords of falsities.
Say it: This is not about selling books. This
is about electricity. This is about a season
of abandon and finding. This is about Saturdays
of unknown proportions. This is about walking
down the same street in different cities,
the beauty and the strange of it. Listen.
Pack light. If you take one book,
take the book by the newly dead poet.
There's a map inside. Or a letter.
If you pack new black socks, watch them
change each exquisite white space.
When you pack a shirt,
don't talk yourself out of wearing it.
When you write a poem, don't talk yourself out of
reading it. Don't be embarrassed
if nobody shows. You have shown. Be
human. Ache. Be journalist. Ask.

Be grateful. Thank. Leave radiant
a copy of your book somewhere you love,
a garden or a staircase.
Someone who needs it will find it.
When you find a book on the street,
put it in your bag. Know it
was waiting for you.

A SINGLE PHOTOGRAPH

I

A single photograph. You and I,
comfortable. Nothing forced
except tired dogs lifting tired heads,
our nieces in the foreground, such easy mess.
On your bluest of nights on the porch
around the corner, a space made quarter-
room with a half-brother's cold feet
and the slow thaw to your own adolescence,
could you imagine a future where this
photograph could be taken? The line of
a family. Your husband. The diagram
of a sentence, a word in the middle hanging
in the air. What is that word?

II

You say the word is miracle.
Miracle can mean so many things
but in your mouth it means survival.
When you were a child you played
in an old barn, the planks rotted,
nails teething from splintered wood.
Your skin was not broken. Once
you fell from the hood of a car into a nest
of cottonmouths that did not bite.
You were raised in a pentecost of
burning books yet you sit across
from me now writing you own.
You woke me this morning with
your full-grown body hammered
against me until we made something
hard, then something soft. Yes.
The word is miracle,
whatever you mean by it.

III

I say the word is life,
and here are more photographs:
I'm alone in every American city.
New York. Chicago. Los Angeles.
We walk through absence like a garden
we've grown in the sky.
Before you the moon never bloomed
like this. When the moon is full
we measure our love by its fullness.
When there is no moon we are
the span of night itself, the immeasurable
dark we see from our own peculiar windows.
In these lonely months we are the oldest
tree in every park. The meals we transcribe
with every swallow. We are a library
full of art books, the faces of friends,
obscene polaroids. I say the word
is life. A better word might be
everything.

HOW TO RIGHT THIS

At night I bury the news like a body.
Like an ax in the back of America.
Come daybreak regretful of my crime,
I let myself know the terrible score
from the arena the night before: everyone
still alive has chosen a side. Each
morning someone I love loses more.
All the poets are dead
because the living are at a loss
for what to say. Everything once certain
is no longer so. An impossible equation.
An incorrect atlas. Entire masses
of continents have broken away.
I ask myself when I look at you how
I would turn these hands to a weapon.
This wedding ring to brass knuckle.
How can this poem defend us as we sit
together on the porch of our home? We kiss.
Somewhere the explosive is detonated.
Somewhere the trigger is pulled. Another
black man dies. The earth has grown so hot.
Some days I'm done with poetry.
Some days it's the only thing I have.

ACKNOWLEDGMENTS

"Summer in America" // *Foglifter*

"Chelsea Boom" // *Talking River*

"The Hour of Common Prayer" // *Impossible Archetype*

"What Else Were We to Do" // *Talking River*

"Chicago" // *Talking River*

"Washington" // *AltResist*

"If You Can Hear This" // *If You Can Hear This: Poems in Protest of an America Inauguration*

"One America Comes to the Other" // *Talking River*

Grateful acknowledgment of all who hosted me on the 2016 *DIG* tour, especially Paul.

For Seth, as always. I love you, buddy.

ABOUT THE POET

Bryan Borland is founding publisher of Sibling Rivalry Press and author of *My Life as Adam*, *Less Fortunate Pirates*, and *DIG*, which was a finalist for the Lambda Literary Award for Gay Poetry and a Stonewall Honor Book in Literature as selected by the American Library Association. He lives in Little Rock, Arkansas, with his husband, Seth Pennington. [bryanborland.com]

NOTES

The cover art for *Tourist* was chosen for many reasons connected to these poems, but especially to honor Adrienne Rich's 1997 quote in refusing the National Medal of Arts: "[Art] means nothing if it simply decorates the dinner table of the power which holds it hostage."

The italicized lines from "Festival Poet" are from Anne Waldman's poem, "Hungry Ghost of Worlds."

"Indiana" is an erasure poem created after my reading at Holy Cross was moved off campus because of my association with "gay poetry." Its source text is "Flawed Families in Biblical Times," a poem from my first book, *My Life as Adam*, which I had planned to read there.

ABOUT THE PRESS

Sibling Rivalry Press is an independent press based in Little Rock, Arkansas. It is a sponsored project of Fractured Atlas, a nonprofit arts service organization. Contributions to support the operations of Sibling Rivalry Press are tax-deductible to the extent permitted by law. I wish to thank the following individuals and organizations who assisted in the publication of not only this book, but all 2018 Sibling Rivalry Press titles. We couldn't do it without you.

Liz Ahl

Stephanie Anderson

Priscilla Atkins

John Bateman

Sally Bellerose & Cynthia Suopis

Jen Benka

Dustin Brookshire

Sarah Browning

Russell Bunge

Michelle Castleberry

Don Cellini

Philip F. Clark

Risa Denenberg

Alex Gildzen

J. Andrew Goodman

Sara Gregory

Karen Hayes

Wayne B. Johnson & Marcos L. Martínez

Jessica Manack

Alicia Mountain

Rob Jacques

Nahal Suzanne Jamir

Bill La Civita

Mollie Lacy

Anthony Lioi

Catherine Lundoff

Adrian M.

Ed Madden

Open Mouth Reading Series

Red Hen Press

Steven Reigns

Paul Romero

Erik Schuckers

Alana Smoot

Stillhouse Press

KMA Sullivan

Billie Swift

Tony Taylor

Hugh Tipping

Eric Tran

Ursus Americanus Press

Julie Marie Wade

Ray Warman & Dan Kiser

Anonymous (14)

www.ingramcontent.com/pod-product-compliance
Lightning Source LLC
Chambersburg PA
CBHW032105040426
42449CB00007B/1188

9 781943 977499